TO:

_____

No parent is perfect — but that's okay, bec
perfection is not a requirement for parenth

FROM:

_____

January 1

There's no way to fully prepare for the cultural
shock of having children. Trying to analyze what
you will do when you have your own children is
nothing like the surprise that awaits you
when they actually arrive.

December 31

Someday, when your kids have grown to be adults, they will travel hundreds of miles to get together with other brothers and sisters or to visit you. Listen carefully to their conversation. If their museums are full, you will hear these words: "Remember when . . ."

January 2

I'm not okay, you're not okay, but that's okay.
Being abnormal is normal.

December 30

Positive memories are a source of strength that can serve as mileposts to help your children keep a healthy perspective on life as they grow to be adults. And the more positive memories you're able to put into your children's memory museum, the less powerful will be those memories of the times of conflict and difficulty that come to every family.

January 3

No parent is perfect — but that's okay, because perfection is not a requirement for parenthood.

December 29

Clearly, bedtime is not the time
for angry confrontation or discipline. It is the time
to take advantage of your child's peaceful,
receptive mind so that you can share expressions
of inspiration, love, and encouragement.

January 4

Confession is good for your own soul and essential
for the well-being of your children.

December 28

Your family table should be like the huddle of a football team — a place to discover the challenges and opportunities of each member of the team, and then to shout your encouragement to each other as you split up for another play; a place where ideas are shared and topics of interest discussed. Work overtime to make mealtimes one of the positive memories in your home.

January 5

Effective parenting is measured not by the changes
you force in your children but by the changes
you allow God to make in you.

December 27

Birthdays and holidays should stand out
in a kid's mind like fireworks against a July sky —
not because of expensive presents or elaborate
trips, but because of the special traditions
associated with those events.

January 6

One of the first steps in learning to live with your kids when you've already lost your mind is to admit that you've already lost your mind.

December 26

It's not the complex and expensive things
that last as memories — it's the simple things.

January 7

Children, in the first several years of their life, form attitudes and patterns that stay with them forever. During that same period, the minds of parents are also being reformed (or perhaps deformed) into new shapes. Parenting causes mental dysfunction. This is one of the first confessions we must make if we are to grow.

December 25

Create tradition together. Memories of tradition don't have to be humorous. Traditions are simply events that happen regularly, thereby giving shape to our lives — mileposts that enable your kids to look back to see how far they've come and to look forward in anticipation to what is coming. Family vacations, holidays, birthday celebrations, and the daily rituals of family life can all become traditions important to a secure childhood and a healthy adult life.

January 8

Any parent who tries to offer a rational argument
that his sanity has not been affected by raising
children has probably raised *too many* children
and totally lost touch with reality.

December 24

Play together. One of the benefits
of having kids is that it brings a new zest
to living. Don't give in to the temptation
to quit just because they grow older.

January 9

Parents who can relax and admit their imperfections are much better able to make the adjustments necessary to be a good parent. Maybe that's why it's so healthy — and necessary — for us to maintain a sense of humor about ourselves, and even to laugh at ourselves now and then.

December 23

Allow laughter to flood your home, and its echoes
will last a lifetime. Someone wisely defined humor
as a gentle way to acknowledge human frailty.
People who are secure in their awareness of God's
love and who have experienced his loving
forgiveness are free to laugh. Humor should never
be used to avoid facing issues or as a weapon to
hurt members of your family, but it should be
allowed to flourish as a part of family life.

January 10

Parenthood is booby-trapped with emotional and intellectual mine fields that are best negotiated by moms and dads who don't stomp around in defensive ignorance. Pretending you're perfect detonates explosions that can alienate children, sabotage communication, and inflict casualties of conflict and guilt.

December 22

Remember the good times. Create a museum of wonderful memories. Memories are landmarks that keep us from getting lost. They bring a sense of security and belonging to a child's life. They anchor deep in the soul and come back throughout life, reminding us of who we are and where we are.

January 11

Not only is it okay for your children to see that you make mistakes, it is *essential to their well-being that they hear you admit it*. Such openness frees them to be open and honest. It frees them to take the kinds of risks inherent in effective living; it gives them the security of unconditional love, demonstrated through confession and forgiveness.

December 21

The teenage struggle for independence is normal.
Your role as a parent is not to fight it, but rather
to recognize its symptoms and help your kid grow
to be a healthy, independent adult. In short —
it's your job to work yourself out of a job.

January 12

Children who don't see modeled, in their own
home, the freedom that comes with confession and
forgiveness may learn to lie, to create elaborate
schemes to cover up mistakes, or to desperately
try to create the illusion of perfection.

December 20

Even in the small things, model in your own life the quality that you expect in your children. Don't give them a reason to mistrust you. Talk about the importance of trust often. Keep even the smallest promises that you make to your children. Parents sometimes feel free to break promises if they don't seem important. But to a kid, *all* promises are important. If you say you'll play ball later in the day, be sure to follow through. If you don't keep your promises, don't expect your kids to keep theirs.

January 13

Our children know we aren't perfect. Every day, they see evidence of parental brain damage and of the inconsistencies in our lives. Our refusal to say "I'm sorry" for those things teaches our children that it is not acceptable to confess sins or admit mistakes. The more dangerous and subtle message is: *Unless I am perfect, I will not be loved.*

December 19

Trust is a two-way street. You can't expect
a child to value trustworthiness if she has parents
who can't be trusted. Let your own moral
standards be a model for your children. No child
will much value a parent's trust after they discover
that that parent has been intentionally deceiving
them. You can't engage in extramarital affairs,
dishonest business practices, or substance abuse
and expect a kid to listen to your lecture
on integrity and trustworthiness.

January 14

Life cannot be lived without making some
mistakes; a life of faith cannot be lived without
confessing mistakes and seeking forgiveness. Your
model of vulnerability frees your kids to take the
chances required to live a life of faith. It helps
them move toward independence and adulthood.

December 18

Teach your child to value trust as though it were gold. One way to do this is by rewarding trustworthy behavior with grown-up responsibility. Kids searching for independence love to be treated like adults, so they'll be glad to be given more responsibility. But be careful. The foundation for trust must be built slowly. The process can be short-circuited if you give your teenagers more responsibility than they are capable of handling.

January 15

**Personal confession demonstrates
God's unconditional love.**

December 17

Even the best kids will push your rules to the
limit during their run for independence.
They have the ability to make you wonder
whether you are the most cruel person in the
universe for even suggesting that they should
have rules. You may doubt they will ever recover
emotionally; you may be tempted to give in.
Don't. If your motivation is on track and if the
guidelines you have set are consistent, stick to
your guns. Many of the crises that seem so
important fade into insignificance in a few days.

January 16

Saying you're sorry teaches honesty, open
communication, and forgiveness.

December 16

If your kids are already teenagers and you didn't prepare them to understand your actions when they were younger, all is not lost. Sit down now and talk with them. Let them express their frustrations; then explain your goal. Work together to decide where you can compromise and where you'll have to agree to disagree. The important thing is to let your kids know your motives for the restrictions you set and your intentions of giving them the opportunity to gain trust and freedom.

January 17

A child who has never seen confession and contrition modeled in his home may have difficulty accepting the grace of God. After all, the beginning of real faith is confession of our sins. We dare confess only when we know that forgiveness is available. As a parent, then, your model of confession and forgiveness is key in your child's ability to comprehend his relationship with God.

December 15

Balancing responsibility and restriction isn't easy;
understanding that one of your major roles during
this time is to help your child move toward
freedom and independence puts the job into a
perspective that may make some of your decisions
easier. Without that perspective, you'll feel as if all
your time is spent fighting for control.

January 18

Your willingness to admit your own weaknesses indicates to your kids that forgiveness must be available — otherwise, how could you dare be so open? That awareness frees them to believe that, if they are open, forgiveness might be available to them as well.

December 14

Your kids need to understand that you want
to work *together* to help them achieve
independence — not to control and restrict them
for the rest of their life. Beginning with fairly strict
limitations gives you plenty of room to loosen up
as your kids prove themselves responsible.

January 19

The first step in any twelve-step recovery program is to admit that there is a problem. Why not admit your weaknesses and confess your sins to God? Then, because you are secure in his forgiveness, you can have the courage to ask your kids for their forgiveness.

December 13

It's important to treat your kids' friends with
respect. If you make those young people feel
welcome in your home, you may be *blessed* with
a houseful of kids that are not your own. It's true
that a parade of teenagers through your castle can
be trying, but it has some wonderful advantages.
For one, it allows you to assess the character
of the people your kids are choosing as friends;
for another, it centers their activities where
you can keep track of what's going on.

January 20

It isn't hard to admit that you're a parent —
that fact is difficult to hide. But can you bring
yourself to admit that you are an *imperfect*
parent? Can you laugh at the evidence of brain
damage so clear in all parents? Can you accept
the challenge to make changes in your own life
in order to improve your family?

December 12

Teenagers feel an almost desperate need to build
at least part of their world completely independent
from their parents, and their circle of friends
becomes that world. The tough balancing act
for parents is to allow teens that freedom and yet
avoid having them withdraw totally from the
family. But you can achieve that balance
by planning time with the family. . . .
Don't give in to the relentless pressure from
your teens to spend all their time with their
friends. Plan times for the family to be together,
and make it fun for them to participate.

January 21

You hold the key to change.

December 11

An adolescent is like a butterfly emerging from a
cocoon, except he keeps crawling back in.

January 22

Confession liberates you in another way:
It opens the possibility of change in your own
life — change that can revolutionize all of your
relationships, including the relationships you
have with your family.

December 10

We must recognize that it is our responsibility to help our kids grow toward independence so that, when they reach their late teens, they are capable of making decisions and accepting responsibility in an adult fashion.

January 23

In the only perfect home I know of, you can look out the window and see streets paved with gold and lions lying down with lambs. If you don't live there yet, then there's room for improvement.

December 9

Recognize that the drive for independence
is normal. Understand, first of all, that it is part
of God's plan that your children eventually
leave you and start their own families.
Matthew 19:5 says, "For this reason a man
will leave his father and mother and be united
to his wife, and the two will become one flesh."
Notice that there is only room for so much flesh.
Mom and Dad are not included at this point.
By this time, we should have worked
ourselves out of a job.

January 24

Most teenagers feel powerless to make significant changes in their home because they have no authority. A parent can come home from a conference or read a book and announce the changes she wants instituted in the home. A child has no such power. But parental authority is not a weapon to be wielded — it is a trust to be administered.

December 8

Jesus said, "By this all men will know that you are my disciples, if you love one another." Such testimony to his power in your life lays a solid foundation for a possible change in your kids' lives. Loving your children unconditionally may be the hardest task for a parent. But nothing you do as a parent will be a more effective testimony of God's power in your life, nor provide greater evidence of your love to your child.

January 25

Use your authority to change yourself.
Nothing will be more effective in molding the
character of your children than for them to see
spiritual and emotional growth in *your* life.

December 7

As you seek God's strength to love your kids
unconditionally, an interesting thing happens:
You will begin to change. You will find that
this kind of loving is habit-forming. Practicing this
kind of love brings peace to your soul like
little else can. And this kind of love does not
go unnoticed. Although you may not receive
verbal affirmation from the people toward
whom you're expressing unconditional love, the
people around you are seeing in your life a
demonstration of the power of God.

January 26

Improvements in parenting techniques will benefit and encourage your children — for a little while. But when things really get rough, it's the changes in your heart that make the difference — not the changes in parenting technique.

December 6

One of the most effective things you can do to meet the needs of your children is to work hard at keeping your marriage strong. Even though your children may never verbally express that need, it is essential to their emotional health. It is one of the strongest confirmations of your love.

January 27

Improving parenting techniques without making corresponding foundational changes of the heart is like building castles on sand. They'll stand until the first high tide, and then they're gone.

December 5

One of the best ways to show love to your children
is to show love to your husband or wife.
Kids who see their parents love each other feel
loved themselves. Don't hide all those little love
pats and kisses from your kids. The younger ones
may wrinkle up their nose and complain when
they see your displays of affection; teenagers may
appear to be on the verge of throwing up.
Don't stop — you are communicating love to your
children as well as to your spouse.

January 28

When a parent is willing to submit to the authority of Scripture and make the appropriate changes in his life, that parent provides a solid foundation for the spiritual and emotional growth of his children. We see our kids — and, thus, our role as parents — in a different light. Rather than using our authority to prove that we're still the boss, we can use it to make changes in our life that will strengthen our children.

December 4

Look for little ways to help your kids,
little ways to express your love.
Because the little things really do mean a lot.

January 29

When parenting techniques grow naturally from our desire to respond to our kids in a more Christlike manner, then our responses will be consistent, rather than always exploding from the emotion of the moment. And our kids will take notice.

December 3

Express love in the little things. Most of us have been tricked into believing that love is communicated only when tumultuous emotions are unleashed or expensive gifts are exchanged. But love is communicated in little things: A note of support in a lunch box or tucked into a school book. A little help with a chore when your kids aren't expecting it. A special lunch or dinner with just you and your child. These little expressions of love carry more weight than we realize.

January 30

The easy part is the everyday give-and-take, responding on impulse to the actions and reactions of our kids. The hard part is making change — changing our responses to be loving and consistent so that at the end of the day we still have a positive balance.

December 2

Don't be disappointed if your "quality time" doesn't turn out the way you thought it would. We often set our expectations for these times too high. If you expect an emotionally gratifying response from your child, you'll probably be disappointed. Kids are terrible at meeting the emotional needs of their parents. (They weren't designed for that purpose, and it isn't their responsibility.) Plan to give as much of yourself as possible, knowing that even though you'll get from your child little visible confirmation of the value of your time, that value is registering deep within your child's soul.

January 31

Often, our first response to family stress
is to pray that God will change our kids.
And that's okay. Kids need to change and grow,
and I would never discount the power of prayer.

December 1

When the opportunity to listen and communicate on deeper levels arises, make the most of it. Make yourself vulnerable; encourage them to talk. Listen to their frustrations even if some of them are vented in your direction. Say the magic words during these special times. If need be, take your child's face in your hands and say, "I love you."

February 1

Prayers are important and should be continued as long as our kids breathe. But those prayers for our children should be supplemented by a more important prayer: "God, please give *me* the strength to change where I need to change."

November 30

Plan activities for that time that you both enjoy. An environment of fun can go a long way toward getting you off on the right foot. Be careful not to fill this time with adultisms and informational nagging. When any parent/child event turns into a marathon of instruction and criticism, the chance for real bonding and enjoyment disappears. Sometimes, just having fun is all the agenda you need. Relax. Enjoy the company of your child — and watch for opportunities to communicate.

February 2

Although we have the power to insist on outward
changes in the behavior of our children,
the most important change we can make
is the inward change in ourselves.

November 29

Please don't underestimate the importance
of spending time with your kids. Make every
minute count. There is so little time available
to influence the lives of our children, and that
time is worth much more than a few more dollars
of disposable income, a new car, or an upgraded
standard of living. Protect your times together.
Clear your schedule so that, when you're with
your kids, you're *with* them — they have
your undivided attention.

February 3

Burn the mental list you have
of all the faults you see in your children.
Instead, make a list of all the attitudes
and habits in your own life that
need to be addressed.

November 28

Search for the hot buttons that unleash
your children's tongues, and then listen.
Sometimes you'll have to sit through a lot
of silence before they open up, but when they do,
you have struck gold, so behave accordingly.
This is the time for loving. And in this case,
loving is the willingness to listen.

February 4

The problem is that we parents find it very tempting to hope that some list of rules, or some application of parenting technique, will miraculously change our family. Deep down, we know it doesn't work that way — but we're still frustrated to discover that, despite our authority to change our kids' outward behavior, we're helpless to change their basic character. Only *they* can change their basic character, with God's help — and they'll be most motivated to make those changes by seeing the results of such changes in you.

November 27

Give them your undivided, focused attention.
And if you avoid (as much as possible) spending
those rare bits of time talking about obedience and
discipline, you'll find that your kids will want
to talk to you more often. Save discipline
for another time. *Quality time is when you listen
more than you talk.* Your ears communicate
love much better than your lips.

February 5

Making changes in the basic character
of any member of the family is something
that touches the entire family.

November 26

Quality time is when your kids have your undivided attention. You can't communicate love from behind a newspaper or with your eyes glued to the TV. Stop what you are doing. Sit down, establish eye contact, and listen.

November 25

Usually, your kids only want a few minutes.
What's more important than a few minutes
that will communicate love to your child? Work
can be finished later. Television can certainly wait.
The newspaper won't rot while you take the time
to talk with your child. And their knowledge that
you love them enough to give them your time
carries weight in the love column of their life.

February 6

You are the only part of the family equation you can totally control. The same is true of your family. You will find only frustration in trying to change the final result without changing one of the parts.

February 7

You may look deep into your soul, learn to love your family in a more meaningful way, and still not see any appreciable change in the behavior of any other member of the family. But because you have changed, the family as a unit will have changed.

November 24

Besides these planned times, be available for emergencies — those times, for instance, when your child just needs to talk. Talking with your children is so important that almost nothing should keep you from responding when they ask for your time. One of the reasons many kids stop talking to their parents during adolescence is that those parents are always too busy to give them full attention.

February 8

You are the only part of the equation that you can control. Allow God to change the attitudes and beliefs that control the way you respond to your kids, and you will have tapped the most powerful resource available to parents.

November 23

You'll never *find* the time to spend with your kids.
You must plan for it.

February 9

I am the key to change and growth in my family.
If you agree with that statement, the next step is
to act on it. If we refuse to act, we won't simply
preserve the status quo — we amplify the
problem. In gambling, it's called chasing losses: A
gambler losing money continues to gamble,
hoping that some miracle of luck will help him
win back what he has lost. This is the reason
gambling is so destructive — most gamblers don't
quit until they have lost more than they can
recover. Now is the time to act.

November 22

The story is told of the old man who found
his grown son's childhood journal. As he looked at
the entries, out of curiosity he compared them
with the entries from his own journal for the
same days. One entry was particularly telling.
On that day he had taken his young son fishing.
The entry in the old man's journal read, "Wasted
the whole day fishing." In his son's journal, he
found this entry for the same day:
"Went fishing with my dad. Best day of my life."

February 10

We need help from sources outside ourselves
in spotting areas for improvement.
We need to listen to our families,
to others outside our families — and to God.

November 21

Very young children aren't the most stimulating
conversationalists, and it's often frustrating
to try to involve them in many of the things we
enjoy (fishing, shopping, working on cars)
that older children and teens are capable
of enjoying right along with us. Still, spending time
with your kids when they are young is an
investment that will pay off when they are older.

February 11

Listen to your children and spouse.
Because they know you better than anyone else,
they can help you identify specific areas
of your life that need change.

November 20

As your kids approach their teen years they don't need *less* of your time — they need more. And to top it all off, they act like they don't want to spend *any* time with you. Just about the time your kids get old enough to make good companions, they choose to spend most of their time with their friends.

February 12

When your family is convinced that you sincerely want to know how you can be a better parent and spouse, you'll hear valuable (and no doubt surprising) "inside intelligence" — most of which you'd probably never have heard if you hadn't been willing to listen. Just listen — it's a giant step in the right direction.

November 19

Your kids need quantity *and* quality time.

February 13

Listen to others. Even when criticism seems undeserved, there's usually a grain of truth. Defend yourself against the criticism, and you gain nothing. Listen to it, and the most you risk, even if it turns out to be inaccurate, is a few moments of pain and a little time lost.

November 18

When kids are asked, "How do you know that your parents love you?" time is almost always included in their response. You don't hear, "Because they touch me. Because they work hard. Because they give me rules to help build my character. Because they praise me when I do right." Even though these are important expressions of love, your kids aren't as conscious of them. But they *are* conscious of the time you give them.

February 14

It takes a strong parent to submit his personality to the grueling and painful search for personal excellence, but that kind of determination can change your family forever. Don't run from the insights of other people. Value them as perspectives from which you can see new, challenging dimensions for change.

November 17

Give your kids the time of day. One of the most important expressions of love involves neither words nor physical contact. It's your time. Once again, don't expect lavish thanks for this demonstration of love, but unless you're willing to spend time with your kids, they may question your love even though you care very much.

February 15

Even when things are going well, grab all the continuing education on parenting you can get. There's a wealth of practical information available that will help you identify as many areas for improvement as you can handle. But remember: All the information in the world is of no value unless you're committed to act on it.

November 16

Many kids reach an age at which for a period of time, they are uncomfortable with physical displays of affection. Don't force it.
You may have to settle for a clap on the back or a touch on the arm as you pass.

February 16

Listen to God. There is no more important source of information about ourselves; we must listen to God. We start by searching the Scriptures; then we allow what we read there to inform us about our life; then we allow God to empower us to take action.

November 15

Humans are designed to express love through physical contact. Unfortunately, we often give our pets more of this kind of love than we do our children. Especially older children. It's easier to cuddle a cute little kid who affectionately returns your love than it is to hug a silent, moody teenager who doesn't respond or even resists your expressions. Don't give up.

February 17

Parents who refuse to identify and act upon the areas of their life that need change are often suffering from their own loss of self-worth; they use their children as chips to win back self-esteem. If you don't like yourself and have never come to grips with your own unique place in God's plan, you may end up *depending* on your family to reinforce and demonstrate your worth.

November 14

"The world isn't going to praise my kids for doing what's expected — so why should I?" That's precisely the reason you should. The world does not love your children, but you do. When you praise them even for simple compliance to your rules or for the smallest positive indications of character in their lives, you set yourself apart from the rest of the world. You show that you really do care. Praise and encouragement register high on the love scale in the mind of your child.

February 18

We don't own our kids; rather, we are privileged
to have them on loan for a short period of time.
It is our privilege and responsibility to nurture
them in the Lord until they are capable
of fully expressing their own personhood.

November 13

Praise positive attitudes and good behavior.
Verbal praise and encouragement are also
important in expressing love. It's so easy to always
harp on the things they do wrong and never
verbally praise them for the things they do right.
But even a lack of criticism is never interpreted
as an expression of love. When a child responds
positively even in the smallest way to your
expectations, lavish them with praise.

February 19

You will never be free to love your children
as unique creations of God until
you see yourself in that same light.

November 12

So if there's not likely to be any demonstrative
response when you say "I love you," why do it?
Because every time you say it, deep inside
your child, another brick is laid in the foundation
of love. And whether your children acknowledge it
or not, your words are filed as evidence
that you really do care. Make it a point to say
those words every day.

February 20

As you experience God's forgiveness,
you will be free to forgive. As you recognize
your worth in his love, you will not need to use
your family to affirm your worth. You will be free
to unselfishly love your kids for who they are.

November 11

Say the words, "I love you." Every day. But don't expect your kids to react with grateful acknowledgment or to return the favor, especially if they're teenagers. Kids of that age just don't do that.

February 21

During your quest for excellence as a parent,
you *will* make mistakes; you *will* fail at times.
Don't be discouraged. Those errors
are the stepping stones to success.

November 10

A loving, secure home base is an essential foundation for kids to feel loved. But don't expect them to profusely thank you for this provision. They aren't consciously aware of its importance. But they *are* consciously aware of its absence.

February 22

Growth as a parent means being willing
to search for input that will help rid you
of negative patterns in your life so that
you'll be better equipped to help
your kids grow and mature.

November 9

Every day of their lives, kids face peer pressure, teasing, and stress whose force we parents have long since forgotten. One of the most loving things we can do is provide a place where our children can rest from those pressures, a place where they are loved and accepted for who they are, rather than ridiculed for who they are not.

February 23

Unless we deal with the attitudes that affect
our behavior, it won't matter how many
great parenting techniques we learn —
we'll quickly revert to the old habits
we've practiced for years.
Those habits die only when
they're pulled up by the roots.

November 8

Provide a secure home base. Parents who make no effort to provide shelter and nourishment for their children will be doubted when they say, "I love you." And I'm talking about more than a house and food — I'm talking about a home. Home must be a shelter in a world of storm, a "home base" where a kid is accepted even with all his faults.

February 24

If there's no communication,
then you're getting no news —
and that's bad news. Even the frustrating
communication of conflict is better
than no communication at all.

November 7

Teenagers, especially, will intuitively test your unconditional love with unlovable behavior. Pass that test — affirm your love even when they're at their worst. If you continue to show love even during these difficult times, somewhere deep beneath your child's obnoxious exterior, love will be confirmed.

February 25

Communication is more than talking.
There are broad levels of communication that we
use most as we talk to our kids.
All are essential to survival.

November 6

When we had rejected his love and were in rebellion against him, God chose to love us by sacrificing his son. *That* is unconditional love. And that's the same kind of love he asks us to have for our kids — even when they're rebellious and ungrateful. He doesn't ask us to condone our kids' misbehavior. He asks us to treat them with love even when they're driving us nuts or breaking our heart.

February 26

Level One: Informational Nagging. Informational nagging consists of giving orders or instructions and asking probing questions about whether those orders and instructions were followed.

November 5

Jesus said *I want you to love each other with the same kind of love I showed for you.* That means *unconditional love.* Expecting nothing in return. Ever forgiving. The hard kind of love. Romans 5:8 says, "But God demonstrates his own love for us in this: While we were still sinners, Christ died for us."

February 27

Level-one communication is designed to get things done; it's absolutely essential in meeting the ordinary needs of everyday life, but it does little to draw you and your children closer together. Kids perceive it as nagging.

November 4

It's always harder to unconditionally love
people who are close to you because you're
so painfully aware of all their faults.
Worse, they're aware of yours.

February 28

Level-one communication by itself avoids intimacy;
it does nothing to enhance relationships.

November 3

You can't be selective with this kind of love; you can't skip your own family and love other people. You practice unconditional love where it is the most difficult: with the people you say you love the most.

February 29

Level-one communication concerns rules
and their enforcement. It is designed
to get us to *do* something.
Unfortunately, it usually bypasses the heart.

November 2

Jesus was speaking to twelve men who had lived and worked together for years, and the first part of his message was that they should love *each other.* Not the rest of the world, not their neighbors, not the people they knew in church — even though his message, by extension, can apply to all those groups as well. His explicit emphasis was that the twelve love each other.

March 1

Level Two: Intellectual Dialogue. Level-two
communication is the free exchange of ideas.
When kids feel the freedom to express their
thoughts, they feel loved and important.

November 1

"Love one another. As I have loved you, so you must love one another." Jesus continued, with words that vibrate in my soul: "By this all men will know that you are my disciples, if you love one another" (John 13:33-35). This unconditional love brings hope to broken families. This love can bridge communication gaps that seemed unspannable. Most of all, this love can forever change your heart. The power of this kind of love is nothing short of miraculous.

March 2

Discussions of faith, politics, world events, and personal philosophy should occur frequently, with plenty of room for questions and doubt. These discussions are a beautiful springboard for keeping abreast of the issues your child is facing. They can give you an unobstructed view of your child's heart.

October 31

Just because *you* feel love for your kids
is no guarantee *they* will feel loved. Your kids need
to constantly *hear* the words "I love you"
and *see* love demonstrated. In fact, your love
for your kids is best demonstrated when you
least feel like loving them. The kind of love that
makes kids feel loved is *unconditional love*.

March 3

Almost all level-one communication is one-way communication. The parent gives the orders, asks the questions, or announces the consequences, and the kid responds with grunts, shrugs, eyeball rolls, or bursts of anger. Level-two communication is two-way communication.

October 30

The adolescent years are particularly difficult for both parents and kids. The complexities of adolescence make it harder for kids to respond to our expressions of love and make our kids more difficult to love. Our cuddly child turns distant and sullen, and we stop making the extra effort to show him love, forgetting that it's during this difficult time that he needs our love most.

March 4

Level-two communication is two-way
communication. It allows for the exchange
of differing opinions. It stimulates thinking.
When parent and child disagree, the child who is
accustomed to level-two communication knows
that his views are respected. He won't hide
what he believes; he will also be more apt
to listen to a parent who is proposing a different
point of view, because he has seen
that listening skill modeled by his parent.

October 29

As they learn to express their anger in more appropriate ways, they will grow out of the fighting stage. Until then, keep calm — and play the peacemaker by insisting that they settle their differences where you can't hear the artillery.

March 5

Parents often squelch ideas that are not consistent
with their own, thereby discouraging honesty.
We mistakenly believe that if we immediately show
displeasure when our children express an opinion
different from our own, our children
will change to our way of thinking.
In reality, all we've done
is discourage our children from talking
about what they really feel.

October 28

We should, of course, strive to teach our children to treat each other with respect. We certainly should work aggressively to discourage any physical abuse in these fights. But for our own good as well as our kids', let's learn not to be gravely disappointed when they fail to live up to our expectations in how they treat their siblings.

March 6

Children quickly learn to keep quiet or simply to say what they think we want to hear; their opinion hasn't changed. And they will eventually ask themselves, *How reliable are my parent's opinions, since he never seems willing to test them against opposing viewpoints?* It is especially difficult for a Christian parent to listen to the questions and opinions of a child when those ideas run contrary to the values and tenets of our faith.

As you react to your kids' fighting
and as you interact with your spouse,
make sure you're setting the right example.

March 7

We parents must remember: Listening and trying to understand the ideas of our children is not the same as endorsing them. Listening gives you an invaluable opportunity to know exactly what your child is thinking and an even more valuable opportunity to suggest other rational options.

October 26

Home is the place where kids can vent frustrations
and know that they will still be accepted and loved.
At least, that's what you *want* your home to be.
Your kids fight because they love each other. It's
safe to fight with someone who loves you.

March 8

Paramedics always try to keep critically injured
people talking. Somehow, conversation keeps
the patient from submitting to the subtle
temptation to give up. Do the same with your kids.
Keep them talking. It will give you more
opportunity to address their strange
and dangerous ideas than a curt rebuttal would.

October 25

At play and in school with nonsiblings, kids are usually under social pressure not to express their frustrations with each other. Lashing out could destroy fragile friendships and, with them, social status. Kids come home, then, with all that built-up pressure stressing the seams of their growing bodies to the bursting point, only to have sister or brother "look at them." The explosion is inevitable.

March 9

If you're in the habit of cutting your children off
when they say something you don't agree with,
you probably don't even know what strange
and dangerous ideas they have.

October 24

Realize that the verbal sparring is less harmful than it sounds. Fighting kids say things to each other that would cause adults never to speak to each other again. But the kids *do* speak to each other again, often in very friendly tones and soon after the fighting ends, strong evidence that they don't view combat the same way we adults do.

March 10

Allowing your children to express their ideas without rebuttal or judgment earns you the right to express alternative ideas and solutions. The open exchange of ideas allows two-way traffic on the street of communication. It also gives your child the chance to move with confidence to the next level.

October 23

Make it clear that disciplinary measures are not
punishment for fighting — rather, they are a
means to stop the fighting in your presence.
This approach can reduce the number of battles
simply by making fighting so inconvenient.
Best of all, it should substantially reduce your
stress level because the battles will be taking place
where you can't see or hear them.

March 11

Level Three: Heart-to-Heart Dialogue.
The third — and most important — level is the
communication of feelings. Heart to heart.
This communication can flow naturally
out of levels one and two. Mature communication
on this level deepens relationships.

October 22

If fighting breaks out at a meal, ask the
combatants to leave. If it starts in a car,
the warriors walk until they stop fighting — or,
better yet, the parents take a break at
an ice cream store, leaving the kids to conduct
private peace negotiations in the car.

March 12

Children can hardly hear enough of words like,
I love you. I'm proud of you. You're special.
And we often need to encourage our children
to participate in level-three communication
with us by prompting them with comments like:
*You seem sad. You seem to be angry. I can
see that you're disappointed.* There is little
chance that they'll respond honestly, however,
unless they're confident that they can speak
without fear of retribution.

October 21

Recognize that the worst damage done by kids fighting is the damage done to your nerves. Since you'll probably never get them to stop fighting, insist instead that they not fight in your presence. Let them know how deeply their fighting hurts you and explain that, because of that hurt, you can't bear to watch it or hear it.

March 13

Parents can learn to use, even in confrontation, a tone of voice that's supportive rather than distant and informational. "I'm disappointed in your behavior. Please help me understand why you chose to disobey," is so much healthier than a level-one response: "How many times have I told you not to do that? What do you have to say for yourself, young man?" Our kids don't bother to give us meaningful answers to questions like that, because they know we're not really interested in listening.

October 20

Insisting that your children attend church
("Why? Because I said so, that's why!") teaches
them merely that you want them to go to church.
Working with your children to discover what
their needs are, and working with the church
to enrich their worship experience, teaches them
that you place a high value on their
spiritual growth. There's a difference.
Your willingness to make sacrifices to ensure
that they are in an environment where they
can grow will not go unnoticed.

March 14

**Level-three communication strives for
mutual respect. It deepens relationships
and invites resolution.**

October 19

It's possible to force reluctant teenagers to go to church, but if we've given them such a negative reaction to church attendance that they refuse to attend as adults, we've done more harm than good. Because the impression our teenagers gain of church is so important, we should be willing to go out of our way to give them the opportunity to worship and fellowship where they are taught sound biblical doctrine in an atmosphere of loving community.

March 15

Communicating effectively with our children on all these levels requires effort — and, to be most effective, it should begin early in a child's life. Even before they can speak a word, kids begin to communicate with grunts, groans, and screams that require acknowledgment.

October 18

Your church doesn't have to feature top musical artists or have extravagant social programs to gain the interest of a teenager. What it does need is an atmosphere of loving acceptance, a commitment to biblical truth, and a program that presents that truth in interesting and applicable ways. And besides that, there needs to be enough kids to make it a group. Teenagers are the most socially oriented creatures on the face of the earth. A church that offers teenagers a loving community of kids their own age who are working together to learn more about the Lord will attract many more.

March 16

Too often, the verbal bombs we parents
drop intending to correct behavior
(such as table manners) destroy instead
the lines of communication by which
such behavior can be corrected.

October 17

Give your kids alternatives. "Make it fun" —
is much easier to implement with small children.
Teenagers are another matter. Their desire
to sleep in on Sunday is often part of their
struggle for independence. Even so, their loss
of interest can often be remedied by the
right church youth program.

March 17

The permissive parent just ignores the actions of her kid; the authoritarian parent allows no response. A more difficult — but more effective — approach is trying to find the balance that allows the communication lines to stay open so that you will always have access to the heart of your child.

October 16

During the week, emphasize the lesson
by challenging each other to practically apply
the truth that was taught. If you make it fun,
you may find that your children
begin looking forward to church.

March 18

Keep the lines of communication open. The frustrations of dealing with kids who have begun to express their own feelings often causes parents to take one of the easy routes, becoming either permissive or authoritarian. Relax; accept the challenge to interact with this little relative. You were perfectly willing to do that when your child first arrived.

October 15

Help your kids enjoy church. By discussing the things they're learning and by asking them to teach you what they have learned, you can help your children enjoy church. Show an intense interest in what they do in class. Young children especially enjoy playing the role of teacher. Take time after church to have them teach you what they have learned. Your interest can help make them excited about going to church.

March 19

Start early and never stop. Show interest in your kid's ideas, and learn to disagree without condemnation. Showing respect for a child's ideas isn't always easy. And it doesn't get easier as they get older — it just gets more rewarding. Far too many parents shut and lock the door to communication early in a child's life. When that child reaches adolescence, we wonder why we can't get it back open.

October 14

One of the most important things you can do for the spiritual health of your child is to establish, early in his life, a positive image of worship. Kids aren't content-oriented; they're experience-oriented. No matter how good the content, no matter how true it is to Scripture, if the lesson is given in unpleasant and unimaginative ways or if the truth is connected with embarrassing experiences your child will want to stay away.

March 20

There is hope. There is always hope. Reestablishing broken communication with an adolescent — or even establishing strong communication habits with a toddler — is a difficult challenge. But even if you've already lost your mind, you can accept that challenge.

October 13

Work with your church to make sure that your child's learning experience is enjoyable. A church that is meeting your needs may be falling far short in meeting the spiritual needs of your children. An adult wouldn't continue going to a church that was dry and boring, but many parents insist that their children attend classes that are just that.

March 21

The lines of communication
with your children are lifelines.
Tend them well.

October 12

Know what your child is being taught, and how.

March 22

Communicating with your kids is
like driving down a two-way street
with no lane markings — a precarious
and uniquely complicated trip at best,
due to the differing perceptions
of you and your kids.

October 11

Ask the right questions.
Rather than reacting with outrage
or disappointment, find out why
your child doesn't want to go to church.

March 23

As your kids grow, they develop a vocabulary
that may sound like a foreign language.
If you want to keep the lines of communication
open, you'll have to adjust not only to the
language, but also to the subtle nuances
of tone and body language (both yours and
your child's) that communicate so much.

October 10

"I don't want to go to church!" Almost all children say those words at some point in their lives. How should a parent respond? Certainly not in panic; seldom is this a desire to abandon the faith.

March 24

If we want to do more than simply get them to the supper table or express anger, it's well worth the effort to find the tone and the language that will help them understand what we really mean and that we really care. Finding the language that will help us find out what's inside their hearts will take even more time and effort.

October 9

When you've made it clear that your child has to suffer the natural consequences of a dirty room, the next step — and the hardest one, for many of us — is to develop temporary blindness. Close the door to the mess and don't look. You'll live longer, you'll fight with your kids less, and you won't be upset all the time.

March 25

Unless we can recognize the moods of our children, it will be difficult to time our communication for maximum effect.

October 8

When things get out of control and your son
needs a compass to find his bed, encourage him by
agreeing to help. This doesn't mean that you clean
the room. It means that you help him get started,
then help him lay out the job in several bite-size,
manageable tasks so that he can see
it isn't going to take him the rest of his life.

March 26

Teenagers, in particular, are subject to mood swings that can make living in the same county with them difficult. A poor grade or rejection by a friend can put them in a stormy mood that garbles any attempt to communicate. As in flying, it's always better to wait till the weather clears before trying to navigate the airways. Don't worry, you won't have to wait long. Sometimes the storm will pass in seconds.

October 7

For some reason, cleaning a badly littered room seems like an insurmountable task to a child. Don't expect perfection. Your view of a clean room and your kid's view are miles apart. I have come, after long struggle, to accept the pile of stuffed animals in the corner as a compromise; my adult preference, of course, would be to see them carefully stored in neat rows.

March 27

The greatest communication tool
God created is not your lips. It's your ears.

October 6

Like coercion, force works for the moment, but it doesn't instill in your children a sense of pride in keeping their own room clean. . . . The use of force to induce a child to keep his or her room clean is cruel and unusual punishment. Force causes more conflict than it's worth.

March 28

We are often so intent on giving our children advice and instruction that we forget to listen; we miss the clues that would tell us what advice and instruction they need the most. And when they've spoken to us, we respond before we've really considered the thoughts behind their words — or else we're so busy thinking up our response we don't even really hear what they're saying.

October 5

How do you get kids to clean up their room?
Negative coercion consists of threatening a
millennium of grounding or the loss of special
privilege (like breathing) until the room is spotless.
Unfortunately, it's a short-term solution and
requires more time and energy to enforce than
most parents have. Even when it's successful, the
room will stay clean only long enough to duck the
consequences; then the loose ends take over again.

March 29

It's hard enough to listen when kids know what they want to tell you; it's even harder when they don't know themselves. And often, kids are unaware of the source of their feelings. Especially with teenagers, it's important to seek to understand before seeking to be understood. And that means that parents must develop the skill of listening.

October 4

In the best seller of all time, The Holy Bible, God
has given us a much better guide to joyful sex.
Pass those principles on to your children.

March 30

Questions from the parent must be asked
without threat, accusation, or demand.
Answers must be accepted without criticism
or interruption. The goal is to discover the source
of hurt and confusion in the heart of a child who
may not even know the source of those feelings.
What looks like confusion may really be guilt;
frustration and stress may show up as misdirected
anger. You'll never discover the real problem
unless you seek first to understand.

October 3

God created humankind in his own image and gave us the wonderful gift of sexual expression. He also gave us some guidelines to enjoy that expression to its fullest. Teach your children to be proud that they are operating according to the Owner's Manual. Teach them to look forward to the rewards of "doing it right"; demonstrate in your own life the benefits of purity.

March 31

Too often, we try to communicate with our children when all our lines are busy; we have our own agenda that keeps us from hearing what our kids are saying. The result is that we address problems that don't exist and miss hidden issues that are at the heart of the problem.

October 2

Our children need to be taught to be proud of, rather than ashamed of, the moral values and disciplines they set in their lives. Just as self-respect and excellence are the products of a disciplined life, happy marriages and healthy, joyful sex are the products of a disciplined sex life.

April 1

Shhh . . . *listen!*

October 1

Our kids need to know that the discipline and self-control possible in our lives because of God's grace set the human race apart from the animal kingdom. We are not merely human animals. We are children of God.

April 2

It's possible for parents and children to say
a lot of words to each other and
not be communicating at all. It's also possible
to utter not a word and communicate volumes.
Whether you're speaking or not, eye contact
with your child is crucial in communication.

September 30

If the human spirit, even with the help of God, is incapable of resisting temptation, then indeed we are nothing more than animals. Those who reject the validity or possibility of abstinence do disservice to the dignity of the human spirit as well as to the power of God.

April 3

Eye contact can reinforce your love even when your words are firm and businesslike.

September 29

One of the best ways to prepare for talking
about sex with your kids is to strive for purity
and commitment in your own life.
Nurture the relationship you have
with your spouse so that it can be exhibit A
in your explanation of the joys of sex.

April 4

Eye contact reveals much about what is happening inside your child. There's a reason you say to your child, "Look at me when I'm talking to you." It's because you want to be able to see, by the expression you see in their eyes, what's happening in their soul.

September 28

God does not restrict the use of sex to keep us
from enjoying it. He restricts its use before
marriage so that we might enjoy it to its fullest.

April 5

How clearly lies show in the eyes of a child
who can usually look at you with unclouded vision.
Shame and defeat are all there for you to read —
but you must look, or you'll never see
what's written there.

September 27

God is neither ashamed of nor prudish about sex,
nor would he expect us to be. Those
who oppose moral purity offer this argument:
Why would God create us to enjoy sex and then
restrict us from enjoying it? The truth is that
the most powerful enjoyment of sex comes not
from responding to every glandular stimulus, but
rather by lifting sex to the place of honor it
deserves: an unselfish (and unequaled) physical
expression of love between married people.

April 6

Although your heart may turn completely upside down at something your kid tells you, don't interrupt the flow with a look of disgust or gasp of horror. If you immediately react with anger or shock every time there's a revelation, soon the revelations will stop.

September 26

Teach the positive along with the negative. Too often our discussions with our kids about sex are restricted to the negative: premarital sex and its possible consequences. We also have a responsibility to tell our kids that God intended for us to enjoy sex within the bonds of marriage.

April 7

You can communicate your concern or advice much more powerfully and effectively if you're careful not to throw up barriers to communication with nonverbal expression that threatens or angers your child.

September 25

It's wise to carefully explain to your kids that not
everyone sees sex the way God intended and that
some are offended or embarrassed by it.
Even though our bodies are beautiful and special,
we don't walk around naked; that's because
we live in a sinful world. For the same reason,
sex is a personal and special gift that is best
discussed with the people you love.

April 8

Anger is not a sin, nor is the appropriate
expression of anger a sin. Jesus expressed anger
on several occasions. In James 1:19, the Bible
instructs us to be *slow* to anger; in Ephesians 4:26,
we are told to be angry *without sin*.

September 24

If you don't answer their questions honestly, they will get their answers from snickering friends and irresponsible television programming.

April 9

Allow your kids to tell you that they're mad. That doesn't mean that you have to let them become maniacal tyrants that rage about the house, destroying property and terrorizing siblings and pets. In fact, it's important not to allow destructive patterns of behavior to continue. Firm and consistent discipline for inappropriate expression of anger is vital as a foundation for teaching appropriate expression of anger.

September 23

The word *stork* should never appear in any answer to the question "Where did I come from?" The amount of detail you provide in that answer will depend on the age and maturity of the child. But be sure to include, from the very beginning, the information that kids are a wonderful gift from God, a gift given to mommies and daddies who express their love in a very special way.

April 10

By looking for the tiniest positive choice
our kids are making in their expression of anger
and encouraging and building on it, it's possible
to progressively help our children learn
to express anger appropriately.

September 22

The lies our society tells us about sex do not beat around the bush — they are direct and aggressive. We must be just as direct with the truth. From the very beginning, kids need to get answers to their questions about sex in a direct and honest fashion.

April 11

Set the proper example. If you're constantly screaming obscenities or throwing things around the house in anger, you're going to have a hard time explaining to your children how to express anger appropriately. And if you respond to inappropriate anger with inappropriate anger, you'll only reinforce the pattern.

September 21

Unfortunately, there are some parents who unwittingly hold on to the old dualistic idea that the body is dirty and evil. This was one of the original heresies of the church many centuries ago. It's just as heretical today. Satan didn't slip into the creation lab and give humans sex organs while God was on a coffee break. We are created in the image of God — and that means that *all* our parts are honoring to him and are there because he put them there. Refusing to discuss our sexuality implies that it is dirty.

April 12

If your children see *you* learning to express
your anger in a responsible and loving way,
they'll have a model of hope to follow.

September 20

The insight that you can give your kids about
sex and love will be more valuable to them
than a truckload of diamonds. But if you wait
until one sunny day in puberty to back up the
truck and dump the whole load on your kid,
you'll probably kill him. You'll certainly make
both of you very uncomfortable. Healthy attitudes
about sex should be built from the very first
years of a child's life. Listen for leading questions;
watch for teachable moments.

April 13

Train your kids to move toward more appropriate ways of expressing anger. The best way to accomplish that is by praising your child for whatever appropriate means he is using to express his anger, and by challenging him to correct one of the inappropriate ways he is expressing anger.

September 19

Make sex education continuing education. Most families think of sex education as "The Talk." The anguish and embarrassment surrounding "The Talk" have provided lots of laughs in countless TV shows and movies. If you try to educate your kids about sex with one talk during their lifetime, then there's no way to avoid that embarrassment and anxiety. Nor is there any way to adequately convey to your kids what sex is really about. Sex education should be more than that.

April 14

Make sure that you challenge your child in bite-size chunks, and praise any progress lavishly.

September 18

If you're not willing to teach your kids about the beauties of sex within the guidelines of God's divine purpose — and about the dangers of stepping outside those guidelines — *no one else will*. Please make yourself aware of the truth and teach your kids how to use this wonderful gift of God.

April 15

Recognize that your options are limited. You can work to allow your kids to find a proper way to express anger, you can let them express their anger in any way they choose, appropriate or inappropriate, or you can refuse to let them express their anger.

September 17

Another major source of information on sex
for your kids is the media, primarily television
and the movies. The media treats sex like a sport.
Morally responsible characters are laughed off
the screen, and almost every relationship,
no matter how casual, winds up in bed.

April 16

Allowing the expression of anger and training for improvement will move your kids up the ladder toward increasingly mature behavior.

September 16

Much of the information kids get about sex
comes from friends. This is like
the blind leading the blind.

April 17

Denying any expression of anger will most surely lead to some destructive expression of anger. You may temporarily save yourself a lot of confrontational grief, but that grief may be visited on you tenfold later in life, affecting not only your family but your extended family far into the future.

September 15

Accept the responsibility. Sex education should not be left in the hands of the schools or friends or television. Not only do these sources distort the purpose of God's beautiful creation, they also unwittingly disseminate some very dangerous information about it.

April 18

Allowing the expression of anger
will go a long way toward keeping the doors
of communication open during
the difficult teen years.

September 14

There's another important reason for
educating yourself: the safety of your child.
Promiscuous sex can kill.

April 19

It isn't only our children's anger we need to be concerned with; make sure you express your own anger in appropriate ways as you communicate with your children. It's especially important that we not, in anger, say things to our kids that we don't really mean. A raised voice isn't likely to damage a child — unless you've been careless in choosing the words you express in that voice.

September 13

It is important that *you* know the truth about sex;
otherwise, your kids will conclude that you're
still living in the age of Fred Flintstone and
Barney Rubble. It isn't enough to be satisfied
with the information you had when you were
a kid. The world has changed dramatically.
The kids in your community, in your
child's school, and yes, even in your church,
are more sexually active than you think.

April 20

When you sense that you're losing control, it's so important to cool off before you continue. Call a time-out. Take as many time-outs as you need in order to keep the exchange rational.

September 12

Most parents avoid the discussion altogether or hope that somehow their kids will be able to read between the lines of "Be good" or "Be careful." That's just not enough. Because of the misinformation they're getting on this vital subject, our kids are destroying themselves. We need to step out of the passive role we've adopted and move toward being a positive influence in the sex education of our children.

April 21

Once the damaging words are out of your mouth, they can never be called back. If you want to keep the lines of communication open with your child, learn to keep yourself under control.

September 11

There are few times when courageous parenting is more needed. There is a tremendous outcry today because the school systems are teaching sex education devoid of moral guidelines. In some schools, condoms are passed out by health officials like aspirins were in our day. We should cry out — but not until we realize that some of the blame for this dangerous state of affairs can be placed at our own doorstep. The true responsibility for sex education is ours, parents.

April 22

A parent has only so much energy. The exact amount of that energy is not measured in ergs or candle power; it is measured only in comparison with the energy of their children. Here's the formula: Count up all your kids, add together the amount of energy they have. You have less than that.

September 10

SEX! There it is, in capital letters, right in front of your eyes. What a nasty word to associate with your baby — and yet during your child's early adolescent years, scads of hormones are turned loose in his or her body dedicated to awakening this drive, whether you like it or not. If you think this is confusing for you as a parent, try to remember how confused a kid feels during this time.

April 23

Keeping the lines of communication open with your kids will require all of that energy and then some, plus a generous helping of patience. There are days, as every parent knows, when it just doesn't seem worth the effort —especially as your kids approach adolescence. I want to encourage you that, with God's help (he has enough strength and energy for all of us), you can make it. Please don't give up.

September 9

You are capable of living the kind of life
that will help build the roots of strength and
character in your kids. *But it isn't enough to just
dream about it.* How you respond to your kids
today is what makes you the parent you are.
Start today to mine the gold and nourish the roots
that will sustain your kids tomorrow.

April 24

Don't give up when they stop talking.

September 8

It is not what a person dreams
that determines what he will become.
It is what a person does every day of his life.

April 25

Teenagers are not generous with their communication. Their new-found independence and the increasing importance of their friends put you and me far down the communication priority list. Even well-established lines of parent-child communication will be strained by adolescence.

September 7

Don't get so caught up in dealing with everyday crises that you miss the nuggets among the tailings. Challenge yourself to be as creative in parenting as you are in other facets of your life. Keep an eye out for teachable moments that may be remembered forever.

April 26

It's tempting during this time to retreat to the safety of informational nagging and neglect deeper levels of communication where we feel more vulnerable. But the sad truth is that now, when your kids are most difficult to talk with, is when they need that deeper communication the most.

September 6

Consistently expressing your pleasure over excellence teaches your children to find gratification in excellence. The reward of knowing that they have done their best can be reward enough. This kind of determination in kids shows itself only in glimpses, and when it does, it must be nurtured and fed with much praise in order to grow. Like the prospector looking for gold, watch for this root of character growing in your children.

April 27

When their clumsy attempts at deeper
communication are met with nagging questions and
negative responses from a worried, confused,
sometimes angry parent, hope soon fades, and they
retreat into sullen silence. Don't give up.

September 5

How do you encourage doing the right thing?
By praising and encouraging good behavior
over and over again.

April 28

Don't give up because your stomach is doing the Mexican hat dance. You and your child will not be able to agree on everything, nor will you be able to resolve all your differences. Accept that fact — and keep talking.

September 4

Teach them to love doing right.
The inner satisfaction that comes from
doing the right thing is another root of strength
and character you can encourage in your kids.

April 29

Don't send your kids from the room or leave the room yourself just to avoid an ulcer. Yes, there are times when you need to cool off before you can talk, but isolation should never take the place of communication. If a cooling-off period is needed, set a time for continuing the discussion — perhaps an hour, or even the next day.

September 3

Waiting is a wonderful clarifier of truth. Slavery
to immediate gratification is the basis of many of
the destructive experiences of adolescence and
early adulthood, such as experimentation with
drugs, premarital sex, and the bondage of debt.
Teach kids to wait — help them say no to
immediate gratification.

April 30

Confrontation can be painful, but don't give up.
Open communication is not only a two-way street,
it's also a very broad street. It must be open
to the high-speed, high-power traffic of conflict
as well as the benign, Sunday-driver
exchange of pleasantries.

September 2

We should help them consider what they want
to accomplish with their lives; we should
encourage them to work each day to reach
the goals for tomorrow.

May 1

Don't give up when you get no positive feedback.

September 1

For an adult, a long-range goal may be five or ten years in the future. Most teenagers can't even imagine five years; they figure they'll be in heaven by that time. A smaller child might find it possible to work at a task for several minutes in order to achieve a goal, but probably not longer.

The average teenager might be able to concentrate his or her efforts for a week, or even for a month if the goal is attractive enough. In a society that thrives on instant gratification, we need to encourage our children to look ahead and to be willing to wait.

May 2

Communicating with kids, especially teenagers,
is not unlike talking to someone in a coma.
But don't stop. They're hearing every word.
Especially those level-three words that
communicate love and encouragement. Someday
they'll snap into a higher level of maturity and
awareness and remember everything you said.

August 31

Yes, it's hard for kids to wait — but the most effective men and women in ministry, in business, or in building loving families are those who have learned two important lessons: First, they have learned to set long-range goals; second, they have learned to wait patiently as they work daily toward those goals.

May 3

Communication is so important to family relationships that it should be guarded like gold. If the lines become frayed for any amount of time, get help. Rebuilding lines that have been totally broken is a difficult and time-consuming task. Don't let things get that far; seek help from your pastor or a professional counselor, and mend the lines while they can still be used.

August 30

Another root of character your kids need to survive is the ability to wait. As adults, we view time from a totally different perspective than our children. Time is compressed for adults; the years fly by. Over the span of forty or fifty years of life, a year is just a blink. But at age four, a year is a quarter of a lifetime, and at sixteen, a year is "like totally forever."

May 4

Keep the lines open even at great expense,
of both time and money. Communication lines
are lifelines. Sometimes the going
will get tough — but don't give up.

August 29

Be fair with your children, be flexible, but above all, be consistent. Following through on consequences for misbehavior is sometimes heartbreakingly difficult, but from those unpleasant experiences grow roots of character that will make your child a survivor.

May 5

If it weren't for discipline, parenting wouldn't be too bad. Most parents have felt that way at one time or another. But the truth is, if it weren't for discipline, life would be impossible. Especially family life.

August 28

If every time a child forgets an assignment or lunch money you jump into the car and bring it to him, he'll never learn responsibility. When that child gets a job and forgets the keys to open the store, you won't be there to come to the rescue, and very likely the boss won't come to the rescue either. Your child's ability to handle such responsibilities in adult life comes from what he is learning about taking responsibility now.

May 6

Discipline is the aspect of parenting that causes
most prospective parents to tremble in fear. . . .
Kids don't exactly relish it either.

August 27

Kids should experience the consequences of their mistakes and misbehavior. Unfortunately, they often know how to avoid this by clever manipulation. "I promise I'll never do it again," they plead. "Please give me one more chance." But the sorrow in their voice is not remorse over having broken curfew by one hour and thereby disappointing and hurting their parents — it's remorse over having to face the consequence of being grounded this coming weekend. It takes every bit of will power not to give in to this.

May 7

Throughout the ages, the cry "There are too many rules around here!" has been repeated a million times. It's been heard in caves, suburban homes, farmhouses, and primitive huts around the world. Little do the kids who bellow those declarations know what a world without rules would be like.

August 26

Give your kids opportunities to serve. Let their
hearts grow tender throughout the experience and
privilege of reaching out to others.

May 8

Although it's true that much of the conflict between parents and their kids revolves around discipline, that discipline is absolutely necessary for survival.

August 25

Nothing will inhibit character growth like never
having to see or face any hardship.

May 9

Just watch the chaos and conflict in a home
that has no rules, and you'll quickly recognize
its value. Better yet, observe the self-doubt,
fear, and immaturity in the life
of a child who has had no rules.

August 24

Build compassionate children instead of conspicuous consumers.

May 10

Total permissiveness will fail because kids have neither the experience, the wisdom, nor the moral superstructure to be able to cope with the complexities of life on their own. Kids need structure, and that structure includes discipline.

August 23

But what a change comes over these same teens when they realize their potential to serve others! Groups like World Servants, Teen Missions International, and the Center for Student Missions take kids to third-world countries or poverty-stricken areas in the United States . . . to help people who are less fortunate than themselves. Many of those kids come back changed forever. No longer do they feel that the world revolves around them and their desires. Their eyes have been opened to a great truth: Value in life comes not from getting as much as you can, but rather from giving.

May 11

Discipline isn't a choice between two extremes.
Just because the philosophy of permissiveness,
taken to its extremes, didn't work is not
sufficient reason for parents to reject all
of its parts. We should not, in reaction, swing to
the other extreme and accept as the only option
an unyielding, inflexible authoritarian approach
to parenting and education.

August 22

I believe in kids. I believe that they're capable of much more than we give them credit for. Yet many of us allow our children to go through life without ever tapping their potential for compassion.

We allow them to grow up with a chronic case of ingrown eyeballs. They live self-centered lives, blind to the beauty and purpose of serving others.

These are the kids who, as teens, consider going to the mall or owning their own car to be the ultimate experience.

May 12

Balance is exactly what is needed here: the proper balance of reasonable authority and intelligent permissiveness that most effectively meets the needs of a growing child and concerned parent.

August 21

Expect the best from your kids — then rejoice
with whatever you get.

May 13

Discipline is a foundation for growth.

August 20

How often, when we talk with or about our children, do we concentrate on all the dirt we've excavated and on the tremendous amount of work we've put in without finding the motherlode. We don't see the nuggets because we're too busy concentrating on the dirt. It's time to start mining the gold in our children.

Consistent, loving discipline will give your kids the
emotional freedom to move toward independence
with safety and confidence.

August 19

The gold miner expects the best. He's hoping for a motherlode that will make him wealthy forever. But at the discovery of the smallest nugget, he dances and shouts for joy, momentarily suspending work in order to celebrate his wonderful discovery. He shows all his friends the precious nugget he has found. Then he returns to work, looking for more nuggets, still expecting the very best.

May 15

Asking our kids to walk through life without the guidelines of discipline is like asking them to fly through the clouds without instruments.

August 18

Zig Ziglar says that we need to look for the gold in our kids. A gold miner is successful because he is willing to discard tons of dirt in the search for a small vein of gold. When he finds that gold, he carefully mines and refines it — and gains a fortune. Have high expectations. Look for the gold in your kids.

May 16

The guidelines and rules of discipline give kids the compass they need to negotiate a stormy world. Rather than fearfully stumbling about without boundaries, they can run, confident and free, within the boundaries. Without discipline, kids get lost; some completely lose their bearing, turn upside down, and die.

August 17

Our own expectations will have dramatic effects on the lives of our kids.

May 17

Discipline is a confirmation of love.

August 16

If you want to build character in the life of your child, start by building self-esteem on an unshakable foundation of faith. Implant in your child's soul these truths:

You are priceless because you are unique.

You are priceless because God loves you just as you are.

You are priceless because of what Jesus paid to redeem you.

You are priceless because I love you just the way you are.

May 18

Your kids may kick and scream, as most do,
about anything that even hints at discipline;
yet inwardly they interpret that discipline as
evidence of your love. There are many signs kids
watch for to confirm that they are loved.
Discipline is one of the most important.

August 15

It is the realization that God loved me enough to give his son for *me* that fills my soul with fire and gives my life meaning, worth, and purpose. This message brings hope to the hopeless of all ages. It brings self-worth and direction to lives that were once self-destructive, hostile, and aimless.

May 19

The strongest evidence that discipline is a sign of love comes from observing broken-hearted kids who had parents who didn't care enough to discipline.

August 14

An understanding of God's love helps build self-esteem. His love for your kids (and for you) was demonstrated in the death of his *own* son.

May 20

To a teenager, "He who is enslaved to the compass is a *slave.*" Period. They don't see the freedom that comes from rules, only the restrictions. So they kick and fight any attempt to establish a new rule, and after the rule has been established, they test it. By testing your rule, they are also testing your resolve — and your love.

August 13

A rare stamp sells for thousands; a one-of-a-kind painting sells for millions. A one-of-a-kind person is priceless. And yet kids often get depressed because they're different! From birth, we need to tell them that their uniqueness is part of their immense value.

May 21

Don't be discouraged.
Rule-testing is part of the
job description of a kid.

August 12

Before God laid the foundations of the earth, he had your son's or daughter's picture on the wall. His design for their life is to make them uniquely like himself — like him in a way that no one else on the face of the earth can ever be.

May 22

There are few responsibilities in life
as physically and emotionally draining as the
responsibility to provide discipline. There are even
fewer responsibilities that will give your kids a
more solid foundation for growth and
development. It *is* worth the effort.

August 11

Joy replaces depression and excitement takes the place of apathy when kids learn that they were created in the image of God.

May 23

Life without discipline would be like a game
without rules — confusing, shapeless,
and you'd never even know if you were winning.
Discipline is hard evidence of your love. It will
save untold heartache in the future, and
it will give you a yardstick by which you and
your children can measure progress.

August 10

For self-esteem to last, it must be built on a foundation that cannot be shaken. Here the Christian faith offers specific hope. Kids need to know that they are more than just a purposeless accident riding a planet to nowhere.

May 24

The key word is *balance*. Every action a parent takes is most effective when it is balanced with another action. And that's not easy — it requires thought, consideration for the feelings of your child, and a tremendous amount of self-control.

August 9

There are no Academy Awards or halls of fame for positive values or behavior; neither our educational systems nor society in general will present awards to honor your child for his upstanding principles. It's up to you to identify those positive characteristics and hand out the statues. Remember: It's not just the behavior you are praising — it's the values and convictions you see developing in your children.

May 25

The rewards for all that effort go beyond positively influencing your child's growth. It is also rewarding to see your own continued growth as a parent as you begin to experience some measure of control — both of yourself and of your relationship with your son or daughter.

August 8

Be on principle patrol every day. Sharing, good moral judgment, proper expression of anger, self-control — all these things should be observed and heaped with lavish praise.

May 26

When we feel defeated by parenting,
one of the reasons is that our parenting decisions
are often not decisions at all — they're simply
reactions to a stimulus, and the stimulus is
whatever happens to be the crisis of the moment.

August 7

When our kids are "bad," we scold or correct them. When they are good, we say nothing. But the absence of rebuke does not register in a child's mind as a positive reinforcement. When your child shows compassion for another person, that compassion should be recognized and praised.

May 27

Our children behave inconsiderately, and we react out of the pain their behavior causes to our ego and out of the context of the high pressure lives we lead. Those quick and careless reactions, besides doing little or no good for our children, cause us to feel dry, out of control, and guilty. It would be better, for both you and your children, to offer them a thought-out response designed to demonstrate the love of Christ and build their character.

August 6

Far too often, we spend most of our time
pulling weeds in the garden of our children's lives,
instead of fertilizing the flowers.

May 28

Effectively balancing discipline and love is one of the keys to raising healthy kids. How are we parents to maintain that difficult balance? By making unconditional love the bedrock foundation of our discipline.

August 5

So how do you and I combat society's misplaced
values and rebuild self-esteem in our kids?
The essential first step: recognizing the unique gifts
and personality of our children. The necessary
second step: recognizing and nurturing
every positive inner value and conviction
your child demonstrates.

May 29

Yes, *you* know that you love your kids even when you punish them — but it's critical that you let *them* know it.

August 4

Our teenagers can't see how valuable they really are. Every minute of the day, another teenager tries to end his or her life. Their very act of attempting suicide is a denial of personal worth. We assign great value to athletic ability, outward beauty, wealth, and intellect, forgetting that ninety-nine percent of our kids don't excel in those categories. We assign almost no value to the basic positive characteristics without which civilization would perish: love, compassion, charity, gentleness, kindness, humility.

May 30

Older children, especially, may be too angry
to let you touch them immediately after
disciplining. But that shouldn't stop you from
saying those three magic words. They may not
soothe your child's immediate anger, but they'll
be heard — and not forgotten.

August 3

The number-one problem faced by teenagers
is not drugs, promiscuity, or alcohol abuse.
Those problems are symptoms of a deeper,
more serious problem: lack of self-esteem.

May 31

Withholding your expressions of love should never
be used as a disciplinary measure.

August 2

Build character on the unique foundation that God created in your child. Strengthen that foundation by encouraging creative and useful outlets for it.

June 1

You can make it very clear that you are upset with the bad behavior but that you still love your child. The proper balance of administering discipline and expressing love teaches your kids that your love is unconditional, that you love them even when they are bad. Balance your discipline with large doses of physical and verbal expressions of love.

August 1

You build the character of a strong-willed child not
by destroying his will, but rather by redirecting it.

June 2

Allow your kids to help set rules and determine proper discipline; it will help them learn sound judgment and understand the principles behind the rules.

July 31

Ask yourself: "What are the unique qualities in each of my children?" Once you recognize those qualities, treat them like a precious seed. Nurture them and carefully direct the development of those gifts in positive directions.

June 3

If you're flexible enough to respond to their concerns, you'll be amazed at the difference in their attitude. Even though the final decision is yours, your kids will feel, because of the process of discussion and mutual listening during the meetings, that you respect them and that you're genuinely concerned with their feelings.

July 30

Build on the existing foundation. In other words,
don't try to make a rose out of a tulip.

June 4

Those of you with newborn children, be forewarned: Shortly after the umbilical cord is cut, it is replaced with a telephone cord.

July 29

Zig Ziglar says you have two options in reaction to
life's trials: You get bitter or you get better.
Demonstrating the skill of positive thinking
can only help your kids get better.

June 5

Bad behavior should never
be a reward for good behavior.

July 28

We need to be more positive in *our* outlook
on life. You'd be amazed how your kids
learn their outlook directly from you.

June 6

Teenagers learn more from the opportunity to set
their own rules — where that freedom is safe and
practical — rather than living according to hard
and fast rules made by their parents.

July 27

We've allowed society to reverse the equation. Real excitement comes from *life* — not from illusions of life. Joy comes from participating, not from observing. Fulfillment comes from giving, not from buying. You and I have the opportunity and responsibility to demonstrate that kind of positive thinking for our kids. If we don't, they're not likely to see it anyplace else. If you allow your own life to be anaesthetized into routine by the tube, expect your kids to do the same.

June 7

Respect begets respect.

July 26

Don't let Hollywood shape
your kid's view of the world.

June 8

Cooperating with your kids doesn't require that you relinquish your role as a parent. Even as you cooperate, never lose sight of the fact that *you* are the one responsible for the final decision.

July 25

One of the best things you can do to help
your kids develop positive thinking is to move
the television from its prominent place in your
home to an upstairs room. Then open
the window and throw it out.

June 9

The attempt to cooperate with your kids should
not become an opportunity for your kids to
control you. Instead, it's an opportunity
for you to exercise positive control
in the maturing process of your children.

July 24

Most of what our kids watch on TV teaches values
directly opposite to those we hope they will
develop. It's perhaps an even greater problem that
those hours spent vegetating in front of the tube
are hours during which there is no creativity
being exercised, no personal interaction,
no love being communicated.

June 10

Relinquishing your role as a parent isn't cooperation; it's abandonment — and abdication of your responsibility in the lives of your kids. On the other hand, don't make the mistake of thinking that a willingness to listen and be flexible is a sign of weakness. The secret is balance.

July 23

Positive thinking is Bible stuff. It's encouraged throughout the book, and it's beautifully summarized in Philippians 4:8: "Finally, brothers, whatever is true, whatever is noble, whatever is right, whatever is pure, whatever is lovely, whatever is admirable — if anything is excellent or praiseworthy — think about such things."

June 11

The positive aspects of working together
are too great to ignore. Cooperation allows your
kids to see the connection between
your expectations and the principles they
spring from. It motivates them to make
responsible decisions on their own — a strategic
skill they will sorely need when they
leave your influence.

July 22

Teaching principles is more difficult than just setting rules. Principle-centered training requires open lines of communication. If those lines are broken in your home, your first task will be to repair them. Only then can you begin to teach the principles that change lives.

June 12

Cooperation makes your kids feel loved by showing that you are concerned about their feelings and willing to be flexible where possible. It gives you the opportunity to see their growing maturity and to reward it with more responsibility. It gives them a chance to respond to you with more than just angry, rebellious compliance.

July 21

Our goal as parents, then, is not *just* to change
our children's outward behavior;
we also need to affect their inner commitment
to principle, the values that govern
the way they see themselves and the world.

June 13

It is impossible to discipline your child unless
you know what is going on in his or her life.
Especially during the early adolescent years,
when kids suddenly become intensely private,
they can make that very difficult. You must keep
your eyes and ears wide open to gather
as much information as possible.

July 20

The rules that can withstand all outside pressure
are those that correspond with your child's
inner commitment to principle.

June 14

This parental need for information gathering runs headlong into another need that is just as important: your child's need for privacy. That need is so important that adolescents will stop just short of killing a sibling for invading that privacy.

July 19

Because rules do not emphasize principles, they work from the outside in. A child who depends on rules alone to guide his behavior, when asked by friends to take a drink, will respond by saying, "I can't. My parents would kill me." As with all outside motivation, there's a fatal flaw in this equation. If this child can be convinced that he *won't* get caught, he *will* take a drink. As soon as the outside pressure is removed there's nothing left to keep him from acting unwisely.

June 15

Since a certain amount of privacy is a natural component of adolescents' expression of independence, how far should you go to find out what's happening inside their heads — or what problems and temptations they're facing when they're out of your sight? Balance is the key. If the communication lines are open and you are taking the time to listen, then your children will feel the freedom to convey much of that information to you.

July 18

Focus on the principles. Being a Christian is the result of an inside-and-out change of heart that comes from experiencing the personal forgiveness of Jesus Christ. That knowledge changed my perspective. Instead of reacting to the temptations of life by saying, *I can't do that because there's a rule against it*, I could now honestly say, *I don't want to do that because of the values I believe in.*

June 16

Excessive prying into every detail of their lives
robs your children of precious privacy
that they need. But just because a little privacy
is good, it doesn't necessarily follow that a whole
lot is better. Total secrecy between adolescent and
parent is a dangerous invitation to trouble.

July 17

The old saying, "Rules are made to be broken," is true only if the rules become an end in themselves and are not tied to sound principles. If, on the other hand, the principles behind the rules are in clear focus, then rules can help build character.

June 17

Let them control their part of the beach,
but don't bury your head in the sand.

July 16

When setting rules, always tie the rule to the principle behind it. A small child told not to play in the street should be told that there's a reason for the rule — the pain that accompanies tire prints on their clothing.

June 18

We should expect these requests for privacy, and we should honor them. Yet in order to fulfill our duties as parents, we should also have access to our children's rooms. And when you enter those rooms, keep your eyes wide open; those rooms hold many secrets about what is going on in their owners' lives. The walls alone speak volumes.

July 15

Rules can give a child the chance to see
the valuable principles behind
certain kinds of behavior.

June 19

Don't ignore your child's room as a potential source for understanding the strengths and weaknesses of your child. But observe a simple courtesy in doing so: Knock before entering. The older your children are, the more important this simple expression of respect becomes.

July 14

Other than providing a stable environment
from which character can spring, rules as an end
in themselves do little to touch the character
of a child. However, rules that are established
and enforced in such a way as to teach principles
can have a powerful effect on the
development of character.

June 20

Establish, so that every member of your family
understands it, that you as parent have the right
to enter your child's room to bring in fresh
clothing (or bulldozer if the room needs it),
investigate noxious odors, and so on.
And once you're in, keep your eyes open.

July 13

Understand the importance of rules.
Changing the behavior of a child with rules
will not *guarantee* a change of heart.
But a changed heart will *always* result
in changed behavior.

June 21

There's an old saying that your sins will find you out. Kids often leave tangible evidence of their sins where alert parents can't miss them.

July 12

You'll be setting yourself up for deep disappointment if you envision the perfect character for your child and then set out to get your son or daughter to conform to that image. The character you envision simply may not match the personality God gave to that child.

June 22

God *is* on our side as parents. He helps us learn
of impending problems before it's too late.
Come to think of it, he does it because
he's on the kids' side, too.

July 11

In the end, of course, your children will make the final decisions about what kind of people they will be. But no one else in their lives will have as great an opportunity as you to influence those decisions.

June 23

Balance being a boss with being a buddy.

July 10

The inner character of a child often seems as untouchable as the end of a rainbow. Perhaps that's because every child has a unique character that exists apart from any efforts to shape it. . . . There is much about a child's character we *can* shape and mold. Unlike the end of a rainbow, you *can* touch the inner character of your children.

June 24

Some experts teach that we should always be the boss and never play the role of buddy. Others suggest that your son or daughter should be your best friend. Both extremes are unhealthy.

July 9

The goal of disciplining your children
is to one day see them value as their own some
of the same principles that you have tested and
learned to trust. When that happens, you'll see
the source of control begin to shift (as it must)
from parent-control to self-control.

June 25

If you make an attempt to be your child's best friend above everything else, you will relinquish your ability to be an effective parent, able to wield authority when needed. If you refuse to accept the role of friend on occasion, you relinquish the chance to show love in a special way and to stand close to your children in their unguarded moments.

July 8

Disciplinary action and confrontation
are usually seen as unpleasant and regrettable by
both parent and child. Try to view them instead
as valuable teaching opportunities.

June 26

Punishment is a method of teaching principle — not a tool for revenge. Keeping that in mind will often make it easier to decide what (and whether) punishment should be handed out.

July 7

For smaller kids, half an hour can seem
like a lifetime. Remember how a kid views time,
and discipline accordingly.

June 27

If you use punishment simply as a deterrent ("and if you ever do that again, you know what'll happen to you"), it will stop being effective when your kid figures out a way to keep you from finding out.

July 6

Some counselors argue that groundings of longer than a week are counterproductive, because kids can't see the light at the end of the tunnel. To them, it's like being grounded for the rest of your life. The result is that kids sneak out, willing to risk your wrath because things couldn't possibly get any worse than they are.

June 28

If punishment is used both as a deterrent
and as a way to teach your child principles,
the inner conviction that develops will stand
even when the enforcer is not around.

July 5

Those of us who have been around for thirty
or more years think a year goes by like a weekend.
Most parents and counselors agree that
a weekend without social contact with friends
is a punishment plenty traumatic to fit the
offenses of most teens and preteen children.

June 29

Punishment should always be carried out when you are under control. The minute you find out that your thirteen year-old son took the car for a joyride may not be the best time to decide the sentence. Twenty years of hard labor in a foreign country may seem entirely appropriate to you at that moment; an hour or two later, when you've cooled off, you'll probably realize that five years would be plenty.

July 4

Make the punishment fit the crime.
Reserve weeks of grounding for federal offenses.
For a teenager, a weekend at home
is like a year with a tax auditor for an adult.

June 30

With smaller children, it's often necessary to respond immediately, so that they can connect the punishment with the behavior. It's still important to keep control. A broken heirloom cookie jar may enrage you. But the child had no idea of the importance of the cookie jar. Express your displeasure about the sneaky action of stealing cookies, then wait until you've cooled down a bit about the cookie jar before taking action.

July 3

Another reason to avoid public punishment is that we parents can't always trust ourselves to maintain control over our emotions in that situation. We're often so embarrassed by our children's behavior and by how it reflects on us that the punishment can cease to be punishment for principles violated and become revenge for our embarrassment.

July 1

Avoid punishing older children (from about school age up) in front of friends if possible.

July 2

Unless the child is clearly being manipulative,
try to do your correction in private.
If you're being manipulated, do your correction
on the spot — and then make it clear that
your action was necessitated by your child's
manipulative behavior. Explain that you prefer not
to do this in public but will if needed.